Two Miles West

Also by
Gary Lee Entsminger

Ophelia's Ghost
Remembering the Parables
Making the Most of WriteItNow 4
Fall of '33

Two Miles West

Poems by
Gary Lee Entsminger

PINYON PUBLISHING
Montrose, Colorado

Copyright © 2015 by Gary Lee Entsminger

All rights reserved. Except as permitted under the U.S. Copyright Act of 1976, no part of this publication may be reproduced, distributed, or transmitted in any form or by any means, or stored in a database or retrieval system, without the prior written permission of the publisher, except for brief quotations in articles, books, and reviews.

Cover pictographs in the Barrier Canyon Style (circa 4,000-500 B.C.) of the characteristic ghostly anthropomorphs, some six or seven feet tall, are located in Thompson Wash in Southeast Utah.

Photographs and Drawings Copyright © 2015 by Susan E. Elliott

First Edition: April 2015

Pinyon Publishing
23847 V66 Trail, Montrose, CO 81403
www.pinyon-publishing.com

Library of Congress Control Number: 2015930978
ISBN: 978-1-936671-30-4

for Susan

O sages standing in God's holy fire
As in the gold mosaic of a wall,
Come from the holy fire, perne in a gyre,
And be the singing masters of my soul.

—W. B. Yeats

Contents

No Fences   9
Steps   10
A Sled   12
Pelicans   13
Music at Three   14
Paper Route   15
Coconut Bluegrass   16
Story   18
Carisha   19
Summer Storm   20
Dream Tracking   21

Return   25
Robbery   26
20 Degrees Wind   27
Infinity   28
Childhood Pleasures   29
Old Bach   30
Bird Song   32
Home Place   33
Gliders   36

Feathers   41
Professor Beebe   42
These Days   44
Alright, Hunting   45
Communiqué   46
Hazing   47
A Private Marriage   48
Fallen   49
How to Read a Poem   50
The Trappers   52

Falcon   57
Easy   58
Spy   59
Storm Toast   60
After the Party   61
O You Famalfudore Scuz   62
Wind and Bamboo   63
Feet   64
In a Place Somewhere   66
Incanting   67
Talking Plain   68
Masks for Kleela   70

Hard Ground   75
Traces   76
Notes to Herself   77
Visions of Johansson   78
Rose Marie   81
Josephine   82
Spring Tide   83
Metamorphosis   84
Kerouac Invented Dr. Sax   86

Two Miles West   91
Clovis   92
It   94
Dreamers   95
Rite of Spring   96
Fugue   97
Blind   98
Keyboard   99
Finally, McQ   101
How to Dance   102
Voices   103
Reading Rilke   104
Window   105

NO FENCES

taking advantage
of saturated ground
I shovel down

around the posts
to loosen them
she rocks

and rolls
them out
now the deer

won't have to
leap
our barbed wire

STEPS

from bedstraw and old traditions
she wakes where blue grama blooms
on her birthday

bunch grass meadows sparkle
a hummingbird hovers
by the hollyhock

while she brews espresso
she measures flour sugar oil
exotic spices for coffee cake

yellow-rumped warblers
nibble the sunflower
seeds she left

she walks out back to
the steep canyon trail
her spade cut

into rain-loosened rock
sees her father
her lover herself

in the work
turning to look
back into the canyon

where the creek runs
by cottonwoods
when snow melts

she bends to stones
fits them
step by step

A SLED

designed and built
by great-grandfather
in Germany long ago

to outlast himself
he put himself
into each detail

neatly woven
fabric seat
and curved runners

years later bought
by a young man teaching
there with his wife

carried to California
and given the attention
of Kane's Rosebud

thrived was polished
repaired and leans now
shining against our door

PELICANS

turn into lady's slippers
alight in the mountains
want to stay but realize
they'll be recognized

as out of the way
strangers in a strange land
disguising themselves
as what

as lady's slippers one exclaims
they agree to nod and make no sound
to remain until lady's slippers
fade in spring

when sunshine bends
and words leaf
then pelicans
leave the ground

MUSIC AT THREE

Grandma rocks
near the stove
I call to her
although it's ten years
since she died
and Moms and Dad
sold the store
twenty years before
I see her there

sky-pours and time
claim no sense
reference images
we believe exist
she comes to me
in full-cut apron
hugging her wide hips
canvas shoes to ease
sore feet smell of
onions and fried potatoes

I ask for munie
and dance
snapping fingers
and thumbs where
the beat purses
her lips
as if to kiss
then pinches my cheek
but it never hurts a bit

PAPER ROUTE

dark mornings
before grade school
walking the road

shadows
of Cherokee
moving silently

along the river
to the abandoned
railroad tracks

where he turns
and tosses
his last paper

COCONUT BLUEGRASS

propping the coconut
between two oak logs
he pokes holes

in her eyes
using screwdriver & hammer
tapping firmly gently

what's unseen inside

while we listen
to guitar & banjo
a bass rapping

he turns the coconut
eyes down balanced
on a measuring cup

the slightly milky
water filling it
& smiles at me

pours the sweet
coconut water
into small shots

toast I say decades later
remembering how smoothly
he orchestrates details

roasts the coconut
until she cracks
and cools her

on the board
pulls her into silky
white pieces prying

the flesh from the shell
with a butter knife
while Don Reno Red

Smiley & the Tennessee
Cut-Ups play
Don't Let Your Sweet Love Die

STORY

this is a story I made up once
about a nurse from Shreveport
Louisiana and a Chicago violin
player they meet
while the nurse is touring
the United States with a traveling
medical wagon and the violinist
is hitchhiking through
Tennessee in search
of a vision

outskirts of Memphis
the medical wagon is stuck
at a bar and grill
jukebox playing
a country song by Merle
the lovers names in neon
Mildred and Harry
I decided to call it
loving you is as easy
as falling off a log

CARISHA

hay rolled into wheels
blue sky tawny fields
stretch as far as she
sees into the mystic

a woman in black shorts
seemingly unsuited
for the work
but strong arms

back lean into it
while men and women
she doesn't know admire
her from a distance

long hair lean legs
smile and breasts
like Helen's looks
past the still wheels

SUMMER STORM

barefoot without shirts
rain
soaking thru

pants and skin
we walked
from Tony's

here
kicking
stones and

talking
football
it

was the worst
storm
of the season

DREAM TRACKING

the first green-tailed towhee appeared
beneath the window she snapped a photograph

male in bright red cap flitting from
straw bale to garden past the bird bath

she: you could be an angel
he: I know how to play a D scale

she: I want you to press a button that says I love you
he: so you were sewing something

she: occasional contributions during snowstorms
he:

she: when I close my eyes I get dizzier
he: and the devil says, well, what do you think about

she:
he: I need to draw more contours

she: with digital there's no developing
he: I've always been drawn to songlines

she: every experience impresses memory
he: expressing everything else

RETURN

upon returning
home from a
cruise to some

far off
place
probably

I was enticed
to see
you

long legs
and
rolly belly

ROBBERY

I didn't sleep
and you remembered
to wake me

it didn't matter
I was already up
making plans

to steal a million
we'd rush out
before breakfast

with our haul
mount a bay
and pinto

ride to Colorado
saddlebags slapping
against hair

and skin
until time
caught up with us

with the sheriff's
posse our butts
in a sling

should've made love
chile rellenos & refried beans
I could'a been somebody

20 DEGREES WIND

I drive home in the jeep
after having an argument
with my girl
one of those
where nothing is said
everything remains ambiguous

like an Antonioni movie
the unspoken things
always getting me
I walk in say hello
every part of her is beautiful
sleeping by her cup of coffee

she wakes laughs
I was pretending to be asleep
hoping you'd go away
I smile recognize
all the makings
of a bad afternoon

the rest is this
unspoken thing
which rushes
past my ears and leaves me
driving home in the jeep
through haunted mountains

INFINITY

suppose Kant was right
that causality is not
an objective feature

but a time space lattice
imposed by a mind
composing images

quicker than you can say
dark as a well
digger's boot

put another way
to contemplate a god
is to see yourself

that the facts
neither begin
nor end the matter

CHILDHOOD PLEASURES

her grandfather & she
a young girl
in 1920s Ohio
walked together
she skipped and scuffed
her patent leather

—don't do that
he said
you'll ruin your shoes
—that's ok
she said
my daddy owns a shoe store

OLD BACH

came from behind the church
and didn't realize where he was

climbed the porch steps
to thick wooden doors

looked into cool still air
nave empty organ missing

rubbed his eyelids until
edges and pipes

converged into an image
of wind chests trackers and bellows

saw himself playing the most
complex machine of the 17th century

saw his final score open
above the keyboards

turned the pages of his
unfinished *Art of Fugue*

knew precisely where
they should go now

inked new grace notes
and his high wire canons

danced into life with
  occult dissonances

recreated themselves in crisscrossing
  harmonies while snow

fell outside his house in Leipzig where
  his children played and his two wives

crisscrossed that space
  preparing for the holidays

  although only one was still alive

BIRD SONG

sad moon rising
as the wind stops
a bird alights
on a branch
we grasp
when we see clearly
collecting memories
for a long night
an iris
a key to the country
that shows
our good luck
raising its head
in fare-you-well
flight

HOME PLACE

Aunt Adeline 90
still loved to tell
of the home place
at the raised foot
of North Mountain
where everyone she knew
gardened kept a cow or pig
traded with neighbors
in nearby hollers
went to town 20 miles away
on a gravel road
over gnarly North Mountain
to Clifton Forge
Jackson River
the railroad
when they needed
something not made
or grown in Collierstown

where her ancestors
had lived since 1786
when John Henry
bought 50 acres
on Colliers Brook
of Buffalo Creek and
had been buried side by side
in the church cemetery
on the hilltop
overlooking the now
almost nonexistent town
where the winding road
still climbs the east flank
of North Mountain
she passed that day

autumn 1936 in a Model A
down to the Jackson River
in Alleghany County
and on into town
she was only seventeen
and married
her sweet man
after trying to convince
the Justice of the Peace
she was old enough
he didn't believe her
but married them anyway
and they all kept it secret
until Mother discovered her
sewing initials
on the pillowslips
she planned to give
her husband for Christmas
there was little left to say
except she'd be moving
to the neighboring holler
since she was married now

GLIDERS

standing in the after
noon grass
wind
rippling at my legs

the gentle noise
of gliders overhead
like snow
birds in spring sky

my thoughts
pass through the trees
on wood and leaf
roads

come back
with reminders of
new poems
bright faces of
friends

the sun eases
into a cloud lake
and cools
I walk on

a thin thorn bush
jags my side
a rabbit jumps
from nearby brush
and hides

FEATHERS

a nursery rhyme
has escaped somewhere
two girls and a boy
leave their houses
run into the woods
live with crows
eat corn get
chased
learn to fly
in time the girls
become crow
maidens and the boy
a night watch
man with feathers
where his arms used to be

PROFESSOR BEEBE

gangling bald
he strolls into the bookstore

fingers slide wire rims down his nose
as he leans across the counter to talk

Slavic linguist professor with a Hoosier accent
19th century aristocratic flair teaches me Russian

while students and curious folk
appear and ask about books

I repeat his phrases muddling pronunciations
while his masterful sounds draw me

a Conté crayon tale of why what how we say matters
he fidgets twinkles and soon has anyone nearby laughing

quotes absurdities from Gogol's *Nose* and *Dead Souls*
while Chichikov wanders the irrational countryside

of 1830s Russia buying the souls of dead peasants
who are still counted as living until the next census

—so Chichikov can borrow more money if he has more souls
and use that debt to buy living souls and make his fortune

—but doesn't anyone get suspicious
—of course the smart ones do

when someone wants to buy something unusual
he drives the price up

or the owner might not sell
—won't the souls be worthless after the next census

—that's right but not everyone knows that
and money talks in every branch of the family

he pushes his glasses back up and turns
suddenly tired as light from a window strikes a cheek

—time to teach he says
and they won't understand his humor

THESE DAYS

Handpick I's gettin' to thinkin' what
you is imaginin' them doing visiting those
relics you been treasurin' for some time
'bout some old time civil-I-zation, which
we is all goin' to be one of these days

referrin' to them
standing at the base
of a statue in another war
museum climbin' on them words
like they was somethin' else
reading this

Captain Thomas B. who led a daring charge
and also wiped out a whole mess of the enemy
before they could gouge him
a hero
 —amen brother

and don't he look good in bronze
I's always said put the heroes 'n bronze & the enemies
become a pack of words in a long time

ALRIGHT, HUNTING

they followed a trail round the hillside
in the morning dark
young men lost
in private matters
one recognized a girl in blue jeans
another someone he didn't love
curios and foggy breaths

until they came to some possibilities
—let's split up you go that way
so he heads toward a ridge
through scraggly woods
rifle butt at hip ready
maybe a little too
cold silent
with everything that's happened to him

wind shivers down the ridge
eyes wide
ready for action safety off
but nothing moves except him
windless noise in his ears
until he climbs out and that old full
morning comes at him

COMMUNIQUÉ

—muscatel, muscatel for sale
a little old man scoots the corner
blue max and forget
hell no on the backside
slides up
—hey boy give me a quarter

a young man startled once
too quickly to speak cuts his eyes
keeps walking forget hell no
isn't surprised
without changing gears resumes riding
looks at whom won't look at him

(stretches his rubber, makes business
of bugging) on to a clearing
where youth doesn't know all of us
or remember itself sometimes
sand oozing
chimes ringing

HAZING

eyes swollen face stretched to cracking
he hangs in the middle of night
darkness he knows despite the blindfold
which conceals his captors' identities
arms extended no longer trying to pull
himself up as if to say no more this isn't true

he breathes silently as still wind
remembers his plan knowing before
this would happen he pretends
to strain another minute then lets go
risking the consequences
falls in a heap in his own country

while strange hands drag him to his feet
threatening further abuses
but when his body stays limp they let him go
as if nothing happened—a game at 2 a.m.
he balances on one foot
slips his shoe on like he used to

A PRIVATE MARRIAGE

you slip the ring
on her
finger

and think
at last
happiness secured

well
when the trees bend
and your shelter

is a ruse
for privacy
those friends

you said you
didn't need will be
far away

and her
be careful
her skin isn't chapped

FALLEN

in a heart beat she had run
to where she had fallen
someone else
not the one she thought she was
and now lay there
not herself

HOW TO READ A POEM

when you sat beneath
the window I stood
along the glass

you nodded
said you knew the truth
of the poem

the wind turned
cold I shivered
I had never glimpsed

the truth before its
closeness surrounded me
a squirrel

munching a nut beneath
a tree scurried
into its hole

head peering
cautiously through
the leaves

when you spoke
of the poet's intention
your voice became

a cold hardness in
my ears
I listened

the water that ran
across the field
emptied into a narrow pool

the clouds
shuddered
at the sound

a wheelbarrow stood beside
our conversation
filled with water

I saw us
trapped
within that space

stepping
over
our lives

dropping the nut
peering cautiously
from our holes

THE TRAPPERS

two faces stood in the wood
cracks lengthened where
the grain gave way
the faces the years the bodies
once smooth like glass
distinct in every expression

separate they thought
yet each was held
within a similar space
cooled by the rain
almost touching
still

altering their poses
to spit on each other
saying we have no choice
have been trapped no
hold on the coolness
so it goes

the cracks lengthen

FALCON

dives
into your eyes
world as long as you
know it

EASY

we pick him up our friend
on the far side of town
in a bar he's not drinking
at least not for his own sake
pushing instead imaginary buttons
that fumble under fingers

my wife doesn't not a bit she won't
understand passes over my 'marks
like they weren't there
or worth her lifespan so I hide
looking for easy but I'm not bad
I tell you (—easy easy Mister Man)

pushed his hair a little to the left
from his forehead saw himself briefly
dropped his hand
withering before you know it
back to the buttons I tell you
I'm not bad (—easy easy we understand)

SPY

on to the clearing where
the last of the fertile women rises
where all will be revealed
—is that you Mister Man
if so you're ahead of yourself
when she revises

McQ's starring as a spy who doubles
as a private eye who's not
only the lonely depressed type
we're used to but also
goes home a loving
little league coach and charmer

but get this
which will spread light
he believes
he's not acting that he is
the man in his dreams
when he leaves the set

STORM TOAST

cloud booms and bluster
winds every which way
the blue sky we're used to
receded into oddities
and orifices turning gray
—full speed shouts McQ

the great orator of long gone
waves a finger we'll be there soon
gather round now and we'll talk
care for garlic and an olive
—it's been a while says he
forgetting is easier now

—so it is says McQ
a pretty girl passes
blond braids sashaying
and suddenly the moon
as she sings to herself
seeing them touch glasses

AFTER THE PARTY

—what a finger smashing time we had
—Famalfudore, what you going on about
acting bewildered as you can
about nine we set out for the big house
McQ driving in his straw hat

someone else riding within
the two of them discussing in private
while I'm riding over the wheels
foot draped from the hood
in high style
if you don't mind the bumps

so we pull up everybody out
except McQ whose calf suddenly
cramps he can't move
so I help him
into the music blaring
still talking to himself

O YOU FAMALFUDORE SCUZ

do you have omens
advice or anything to retrieve
—well if it fits
McQ walking on a highway
gets 'em all in an announcement
—I've been saving up
he says to have something you'll follow
(not need or want keep close to that)

listening up they get in line
and follow McQ as the highway curves
between groves of sycamore locust
and dogwood shading marshy undergrowth
McQ in front chants a rousing cadence
which echoes down the line
onto a crossing after a few miles
—I have to go back now you're on your own

at first bewilderment then a sinking
although some shout encouragement
while others complain about the heat
that previously had not been felt
followed by getting lost talk without McQ
to guide them and momentum leads
to that old familiar restlessness
erupting again from fallen leaves

WIND AND BAMBOO

in Henry Evans' print
Black Bamboo
feathery green leaves
sway
across black culms
as if the wind's
come to town

flute-like stalks
bend
into smooth white chord
invisible bare feet
finger light dancing
a small ensemble
of contours

FEET

a woman I've seen before
lies where the grass
leans from a shore
in photosynthesized air
reading *Anna Karenina*
turns a page
as he approaches
on his way somewhere

her ankles cuffed
by wrinkled pants
toes wiggle out to dance
teasing his stockings
bringing his fleet full stop
he lights a smile
suddenly aware of her
harbor a commodore

you should have seen his teeth
should have been there
when he found
the sweet sparkle
noticing him
his feet close enough now
to consider
what it means

remembering others before
ones he wanted to meet
the times he'd heard
his uncle repeat the orator
feet to feet
watch your step
no need to dash
down the corridor

IN A PLACE SOMEWHERE

I have opened them all
they lie opened
on the table the couch
the desk the piano
and crawl up the back
of the rocker
where Grandma sat
what to do with them
that's the question

she sang hymns
about rocks of ages
as I cried for more
the road in front of the store
where Dad extended credit
he couldn't afford
two-laned in those days
east to town west to North Mountain
where the communes came and went

and now I-64 bypasses
all of them
the store and Grandma
no longer exist
but memory interrupted
no longer exists
azalea fills the basket
wind and bird coexist
sweep clean the breakfast

INCANTING

I'm standing at my door
imploring the sky for him
whose leaving was a crime
unlike love

I try forgetting
that I washed his feet
that his words stirred anything
when I recall his blood

I don't I haven't
although he said I would
he deserts himself not me
I've said I'm done

soon I'll cross him out easily
shadows full of worms
leave my fire
go where the work is

let him hallucinate
freedom
take him straight
to the devil

TALKING PLAIN

it's been how many
—41 years
that so
I don't have much to show for it
rights to a few more
or less they say

smell that air last night
inversion
skunk to high heaven
which isn't so high anymore
magic moonbeam collectable
buy a copy cheap at the store

I hold my piece
of ground whether they want
me to stay or not
engines rev the main drag
but it's mostly quiet
this far up the dead-end

two kids in the next yard
wrapped wintry fight over
—leave me alone
—mine
where the sun strikes
a fallen pine

the neighbor's dog
howls from three feet of cord
strangling himself
I'd yell then the dog gets his
and a while later
howling again

I've tried talking plain
no one listens
empty-headed better to string 'em up
now than to feed them
through this beastly period
I grumble now more than I used to

MASKS FOR KLEELA

at night I pull the one runner curtain back
and look out the porch caves into ruined couch
below unshingled casts from lamplight

shadows of upholstery I stare out
in land age-pocked and graying and don't know what
you're running down

moonlight and stars don't argue for grass
the patch of park where the street breaks
into vulnerable banks

we're responsible I close automatically
step up on well-tested stairs toward bed
as if heaven awaits

HARD GROUND

he crossed an open place he
saw once in a dream quite
clearly three crows one fly

held his path the crows
forming triangles drawing straight
lines from their beaks

he approached the fly I
used to be a bird he said and
grew tired the fly sat quietly

what he noticed he never
let on
the crows dipped their heads

intermittently into hard
ground
he passed them

TRACES

wind sweeping
slick rock
how far does it wend

through how many
canyon bends
can we experiment

toss a raven's
feather into the air
and follow

until we reach its lair
and find the feather
carried there

in this expanse
of ancient spans
and introspection

we see ourselves
microscopic
in the distance

a scrub jay
hops through
our campsite

knowing
we've left traces
of what we eat

NOTES TO HERSELF

a young woman
hunched over a desk

dim light quiet
corner of the library

stops her pen eyes rise
from notes to herself

left arm holding
the book down

while her pen thumps
two beats rain falling

as she wonders
if he's gone home

has started contemplating
their dinner

in the little kitchen
bedroom studio

where other married
students like them

bed down
imagine their futures

larger rooms
more options

VISIONS OF JOHANSSON

Sixty Things To Do
When You're Celebrating Sixty

be with you
don't mind us
forget the fuss
have fun
ski run

imagine Quebec
eat French cuisine
listen to gypsies
sit lakeside in moonlight
dance outside on a warm night

learn Mayan
go to Peru
climb to your temples
breathe deeply
eat beans & tortillas

go to Colorado
hike up Copper Creek
soak in the hot springs
camp at Lost Lake
drink water

listen to Kerstin
advise Nick
confide in Ali
heal the sick
laugh with everyone

sit quietly with CP
party with the Grateful Dead
fly high with the Byrds
sing with Elvis
sing with g & Susan

do downward dog & cobra
sleep tight
get a massage
give a massage
look into someone's eyes tonight

smell a rose
plant garlic
water tomatoes
rearrange stones
create a forest

have visions
dream about paradise
relax on a beach
wonder why canyons drift
imagine your dad and mom

learn to play harmonica
build a desk
read *On the Road* again
gather wood for winter
batten the hatches

Gait of Power into the night
knees up back straight
relax at home
dig the earth
dig it yes yes

imagine you're 60
accept a toast
eat some toast
scramble eggs
it's you the best

ROSE MARIE

the image of a group circled
reappeared and this time she noticed
as much as she could before it faded

again she didn't recognize the place
faces hazy acquiring possible names only
when she suggested them herself

then she saw someone alone
sitting in golden grass on a high hillside
face familiar but no one

in the distance a marching
band's drums and horns wind lifting
her dress arms balanced on knees

she scribbled questions where
do they come from do they belong
to me and no one else

why now that one a circle
inside a place perhaps a dwelling
then a hillside the rest hidden

waiting to be summoned

JOSEPHINE

we have
not seen
today

she must be
in the orchard
with a basket

picking apples
trees pulsing
her veins

and roundness
come come
my dear

we'll eat and sing
share the night
with Josephine

SPRING TIDE

when the moon
is full or new
tides are high

the unfolding roar
at the shore
as gulls flail

waves crashing
into frothy edges
where a lone surfer

too far out rides
turns glides
and disappears

board buoyed
while the watcher
waits for a sign

METAMORPHOSIS

they knew
to go higher

wherever they were
step up

if in a valley
climb to the ridge

below a summit
try to reach one

perhaps you will
need a rope

at the base
of steep cliffs

waves crashing
into tide pools

of starfish
anemone and sponge

below the dunes
work your way up

through the maze
of slick rock

to find
the wooly bears

crossing sandy paths
always in the same direction

one day to the next
climbing higher

to just below
somewhere else

soon to become
tiger moths

KEROUAC INVENTED DR. SAX

to explain the ghost
who appears in the woods
and sidles the dark

shadows and byways
of churches funeral
parlors and cemeteries

the beat drawing him in
Bird Diz Coltrane
Billie Holiday

music
he knows
by heart

and reminds himself
as he begins to sleep
to note carefully

his dreams the friends
and other ghosts
he finds there

Jack's ghost noted mine
64 years ago in 1950
when he heard the bird

of Shenandoah and stepped
from the bus to see
Stonewall Jackson's grave

while I was being born
in Jackson's old brick home
become hospital

a mile from the cemetery
Stonewall was 29
when he was wounded

by friendly fire in 1863
87 years to the day
before I was born

Jack was 28
and back on the bus
by dusk heading west

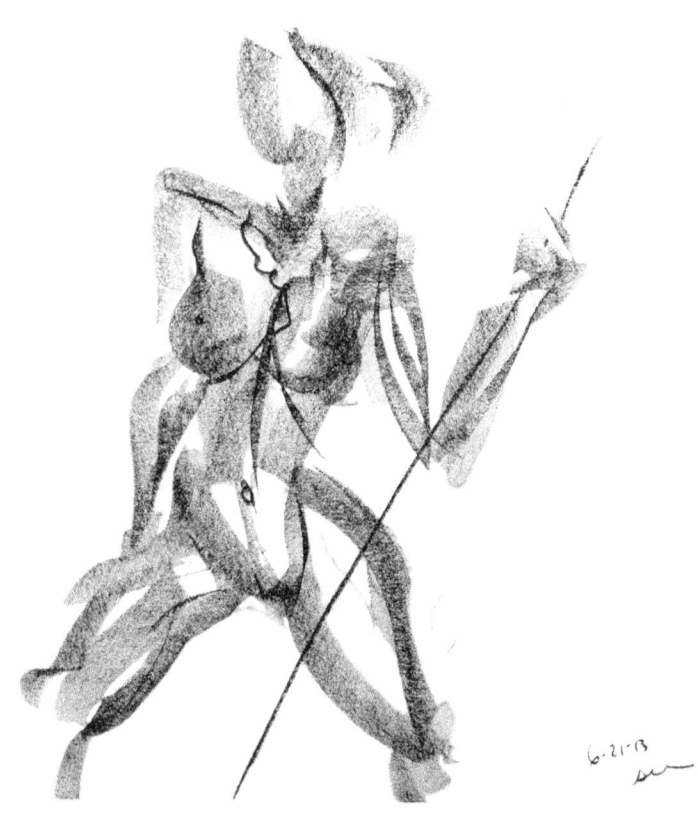

TWO MILES WEST

we've all been
down that road
leaving town

a neon glaze
coming up
on the right

we're tempted
to stop go inside
order a beer

or other intoxication
the woman in the booth
intrigues anyone

who notices
disappointment
I see it in your eyes

should we not
go there focus instead
on the drive

the fields passing
where beets prepare
for morning

CLOVIS

corn had been harvested
leaving the brown fields
bare by the river

ancient ones
we recognize
as ourselves

yet we believe them
more primitive
hunters gatherers

women bathing
in the river
men watching

from higher rocks
chipping their distinctly
honed projectiles

which we find
in the fields
just before sunset

giddy with our discovery
of something
lost

13,000 years ago
when these Paleo-Indians
roamed

most of the Americas
and lived here
as well as we

can know
from what we find
by the river

IT

in a dark
seedy side
what he doesn't know
shivers in a blanket

having crossed
the silence
it stops
hearing him

lacking
the tools
to get on in the world
ghostly strangers

—remember
—I try
child dreaming
in the dark

faces him
but it has no face
until he awakens
in someone's arms

DREAMERS

circle
the sky wet
with chances

tapping
into the belly
spirit

chanting
a tune
we all know

but who remembers
how we
used to dance

each day
attentive
to our goddesses

Ishtar Isis Coca
Venus Aphrodite
slept well each night

RITE OF SPRING

we long
to be closer
to the trees

sky rock
as we roll
into the park

campground
full of RVs
vroom vroom

give us room
to propagate
our mischief

as we evolve
into hip incarnations
of bourgeoisie

compositions
of irregular beats
gongs shorts and longs

horn beeps
as we lock up
in the twilight

a scrub jay alights
where I find a penny
heads up at our site

FUGUE

from dirt to sky
each day more concretized
pavement and perks
shadow the flow
of qi into our hearts
where good
and evil starts

once we breathed easier
the sky open
and we were ourselves
aware of what we couldn't see
but knew in our hearts
where good
and evil starts

when did we come
to make so much
of what we bought
when we knew
within our hearts
where good
and evil starts

great horned owl hoots
cock crows first light
come close caress
the breast where dreams
dwell within our hearts
before good
and evil starts

BLIND

eyes burned out
he'd had enough
storms into the night
strikes straight for the woods
fresh dogwood smell
birds old wet logs

not long after rain
until
a clearing of orchard
grass finds a dry spot
looks out
into himself

images eyeballing his
eyelids two women
in tight jeans
rise up
laughing slip
a ways farther

is this where he belongs
wants to follow
know paradise
among the apples
leans a ladder
and climbs

KEYBOARD

Beethoven's daringly
spaced notes
turn upon themselves
as if Chubby Checker
had walked into the room
and said let's eat

Louie Van echoes
—we'll recapitulate
after the feast
but I tell you now
we'll move between
twos and threes

shaking our booties
and twisting again
like we did last summer
—Louie, Chubby says
where did we meet
you were older then

—Chubby, Louie Van replies
they all try to cheat
us be wise shall I play something
and goes to the piano
in a grand mode
fingers several Lydian glides

up and down the keyboard
as Chubby sways while humming
—like we did last year
and Louie Van says
—you know I can't hear
but I feel it coming

FINALLY, MCQ

what did you expect anyway
to be laid low
and quick and early
or sunbursts at seven
clouds disappearing
mountains within reach

she sits on rumpled sheets
window without glass
lets in cool air
and parts her long hair
plays on her pale nape
all through the rest of the house

everyone sleeping
after a long night
shouting and drinking
resting now in sunlight
after morning mist
rocks still wet

HOW TO DANCE

she writes in a language
I do not know
although my own
left meaningless
relearns how to dance
among her certain
words and phrases
where goddesses misbehave
unswayed by chance
intention prayer

VOICES

—you got that Handpick
or would you rather hear
what I truly think

voices what good are they
better to have a roll in the hay
with someone you love
or want to

—who counts coup nowadays
—not I McQ
what good would it do
let's agree and Handshake

READING RILKE

by the campfire
in the twilight
a coyote

steps from boulders
above us
peers into the valley

why weren't
we comfortable
with paradise

I make a note
as the cottonwood crackles
where are the angels

we fare no better now
in our interpreted worlds
beneath the higher stars

still as terrified
yet if we beckon
will they reappear

as themselves
and will we recognize
our past echoes in their wings

WINDOW

you are bread
and the hairline noise
of flesh and bone

almost
the sea
but not stone

or molten sound
have no hands
yet see

this kind of bird
flies backward
and this love

breaks
on a window
pane where no light

talks of not the time
for crossing tongues
sand here never shifts

I think tomorrow
turned you
with her toe

and you shine unspent

www.ingramcontent.com/pod-product-compliance
Lightning Source LLC
Chambersburg PA
CBHW021016090426
42738CB00007B/805